You Can Read Ja

MW01013311

Short Stories
for Japanese
Learners

-The Red Candle-

Beginner-Friendly Fun and Engaging Stories to Expand

Your Vocabulary and Kanji Knowledge!

JAPANESE LANGUAGE PARK

You Can Read Japanese!

First Edition June 2022

ISBN 9798806215230

Simplify Translation: Kazuhiko Oki / Yumi Nishino

English Translation: Alessandro Easthope

Illustration: Valery Vell

Leveling Guide: Based on the guidelines at NPO Tadoku, tadoku.org.

LET'S READ JAPANESE!

You Can Read Japanese! series helps you by guiding you through fun, engaging stories on your Japanese learning adventure. This book uses proven learning methods of native speakers to help you acquire language skills. By reading these stories, you'll acquire useful and common Kanji effectively without resorting to writing drills. Easily use this guide to discover your own level of learning by starting with easy stories and finding your own strengths and weaknesses.

Level 1 **Introductory Level**
Suitable for new learners who have learned Hiragana and Katakana and are able to read short sentences in simple grammar.

Level 2 **Pre-Intermediate Level**
Suitable for learners who can understand basic phrases and language structure in addition to reading slightly longer sentences.

Level 3 **Intermediate Level**
Ideal for learners who can understand complex grammar and vocabulary and read long passages with ease.

Level 4 **Advanced Level**
Ideal for learners who can understand honorifics, conversations in near native Japanese and can read Kanji without Furigana.

Level 5 **Native Level**
Suitable for learners who are able to follow abstract writings and idioms, finally helping in reading general books.

Japanese Language Park will provide you with new vocabulary in familiar settings, making it easy to understand new phrases and combinations with exciting stories spanning multiple genres.

Visit https://jplgpark.com for more information.

CONTENTS

YOUR FREE GIFT

You Can Read Japanese! LEVEL 1
Essay - It's That Easy!

To pick up your FREE Japanese book, visit here:

https://gift.jplgpark.com/first-essay

What You'll Find

- A book of five Japanese essays, geared towards beginners
- Stories written using simple grammar, some including illustrations
- Written in "です／ます" form used in conversation, perfect for first time readers
- All Katakana and Kanji have Furigana, making it possible to read each story without needing a dictionary
- Funny, interesting stories with audio
- Both Japanese and American-style simple essays, made to be understood easily

INTRODUCTION

Learning Japanese is one of the most rewarding feats a native English speaker can accomplish. With over 1000 Kanji, each with multiple readings, it can be daunting to get started, but that's where we come in! **You Can Read Japanese!** series can help unstick you from just textbooks and guide you towards reading normal Japanese books.

We know that there are a lot of resources provided for people to learn Japanese, but many can be disjointed and feel like swimming blindly through the ocean. That's why we exist. By providing a simple path for you to follow, we'll guide you through your journey towards understanding like a natural.

It can be a lot of fun learning through reading fun Japanese manga, and it's a great resource! However, they often contain unique slang and uncommon usage of certain phrases, which out of context can sound strange to native Japanese speakers. To help you get a sense of what fits best, this book contains numerous short stories for you to get your feet wet.

Features of this series:

- **Written Japanese restricted by level** for ease of understanding, including gradually increasing levels of grammar and vocabulary as you rise from Level 1(Introductory) to Level 5(Native).

- **Ten fun and interesting stories**, including several different genres and styles. From Comedy to Horror all the way to Sci-Fi, you're sure to find something just for you!

- **All stories written by native Japanese authors**, including famous classic authors such as Nankichi Niimi and Kyusaku Yumeno.

- **An illustration** for each story to help you immerse yourself easier.

- Includes **reading comprehension questions** to quiz yourself on your understanding level.

- For things you don't understand, yet, there are **English translations** and including translations for new words and phrases. This helps to provide a continuous improvement of your skills even as you engage.

- Each story is a **suitable length** to help you improve, while also providing a feeling of accomplishment once you finish.

- **A perfect number of stories** to keep you engaged without the feeling of being buried under a pile of books.

THE 5 TIPS FOR EFFECTIVE EXTENSIVE READING

What is Extensive Reading? As the name suggests, it's really just reading a lot. Extensive reading is the act of reading a connected story to gain a better understanding of words in context. This is more beneficial than reading disconnected phrases in study guides.

Here are some tips:

1. **The more you find enjoyment in reading, the more you will read.** The more you read, the more your vocabulary will grow. Try to pick up and read stories that match your interests and needs.

2. **You don't need to understand everything.** If you find a word you don't know, consider yourself lucky to have it as a chance to grow. Try to guess its meaning. Words used repeatedly may be essential words you can guess from the context.

3. **Reading achievement is important.** Setting goals can help you feel more positive. You'll get great results. For example, set a goal: "If I can read one story within 30 minutes, today's reading challenge is a success."

4. **Share your goals with your friends or family.** Share your learning plan on social media. Sharing your goal will significantly increase your motivation.

5. **Reading is input, so the next step is output.** It will help you understand the content better and help you retain the knowledge you have acquired through reading. It is recommended that you write a book report that describes the story in your own words and connects it to your feelings.

Of course, these are all things you might remember from when you learned to read your native language. You'll carry those same tips into your Japanese studies, because although it may be very different from English, Japanese is just another language. Things like this can help to demystify the language, despite its numerous challenges and differences.

THE 6-STEPS FOR READING EFFECTIVELY

Now that you're more familiar with tips for extensive reading, remember to make your reading as effective as possible. If faced with twenty minutes of staring at the page versus ten minutes of targeted studying, you're sure to guess which is more effective.

✓ **Step 1**: Look at the title and the illustration and guess what will happen.

✓ **Step 2**: Read through the first time. When you see unfamiliar words, try to guess the meanings.

✓ **Step 3:** Read through the story a second time and check your understanding.

✓ **Step 4**: Check the vocabulary list for words you weren't familiar with. See if it matches your contextual guess.

✓ **Step 5**: Take the quiz and answer the questions. It's okay if you make mistakes, it will deepen your understanding.

✓ **Step 6**: Finally, write a review of the story in your own words. You may want to write down your feelings on the story to help solidify your memory.

While you're at it, **don't forget to check out the audiobook!** Remember that memory works by creating different "pathways" for your brain to access information. Both visual and audio are ways to do that effectively. Listening to an audiobook will help your own spoken pronunciation and help you get used to hearing properly pronounced Japanese. An absolute must for learners of any level!

Translator's Note

When I was translating these short stories, there were times when I chose to prioritize easier expressions or syntax that was closer to the original Japanese over something that may have been more natural but difficult. I did this so the reader could more easily compare and contrast the two languages and get the most educational value from it.

There are a few discrepancies you may notice. For example, in Japanese it's common to jump around from present to past tense or from first person to third person when telling a story. I found that to sound too unnatural in English and avoided that.

I believe these will be very enjoyable and useful stories to help you learn. I encourage you to think about the differences between the Japanese and English and alternate ways of wording things. It will help you on your language learning journey! Please enjoy reading this book.

The Red Candle

赤い蝋燭
あか　　ろうそく

ある日、猿が、山から村の方へ遊びに行くと、赤い蝋燭が一本ありました。赤い色の蝋燭を見たことがありませんでしたから、猿はその蝋燭を花火だと思いました。

猿は、赤い蝋燭を山へ持って帰りました。そして、とても大切にしました。

山のみんなはびっくりしました。鹿も、猪も、ウサギも、亀も、イタチも、タヌキも、狐も、まだ一回も見たことがないからです。

「それは何？」

「ほう、きれいだね」

「これは、すごい」

鹿や、猪や、ウサギや、亀や、イタチや、タヌキや、狐は、押し合って赤い蝋燭を見ました。すると猿が、

「あぶない、あぶない。これは花火ですから、近づくと爆発するよ」と言いました。

「わぁー！」

みんなは、急いで遠くへ行きました。

猿は、花火がとても大きな音がして、とてもきれいに空に上がる、とみんなに教えてあげました。

「花火はそんなにきれいなの？」みんなは、花火を見たいと思いました。

「じゃあ、今晩、山の一番上で花火を打ち上げましょう」と猿が言いました。みんなはとても喜びました。そして、花火のことを思って、うっとりしました。

夜になりました。みんなは、わくわくしながら山の一番上に着きました。

「さあ、花火を打ち上げましょう」でも、困ったことがありました。誰も火を付けないのです。みんな、花火を見たいのですが、火が好きではありませんでした。

「これでは花火が上がりませんので、火を付ける人を、くじで決めましょう」

最初は、亀になりました。亀は、元気を出して花火の方へ行きました。でも亀は、花火のそばに来ると、首が出て来なくなりました。

もう一回くじを引きました。次は、イタチです。
イタチは、目が悪いですから、蝋燭の周りをうろうろす
るだけでした。

それを見ていた猪は、前に出ました。猪は、勇気があり
ます。すぐに花火のところへ行きました。そして、
本当に火を付けました。

みんな、びっくりして隠れました。そして、耳を塞ぎま
した。耳だけではありません。目も塞ぎました。

「‥‥‥‥‥‥」

何も音がしません。蝋燭は、静かに静かに燃えているだ
けでした。

VOCABULARY LIST · 単語リスト

- 猿/ *saru* / monkey
- 蝋燭/ *rōsoku* / candle
- 花火/ *hanabi* / fireworks
- 近づく/ *chikazuku* / to approach, to get closer
- 爆発する/ *bakuhatsusuru* / to explode
- 打ち上げる/ *uchiageru* / to launch
- うっとりする/ *uttorisuru* / to be entranced
- わくわく/ *wakuwaku* / to be excited
- くじ/ *kuji* / lot
- 決める/ *kimeru* / to decide
- 首/ *kubi* / neck
- 周り/ *mawari* / surroundings
- うろうろする/ *urourosuru* / to wander around
- 勇気/ *yūki* / courage
- 隠れる/ *kakureru* / to hide
- 塞ぐ/ *fusagu* / to block, to cover
- 燃える/ *moeru* / to burn

QUESTIONS・問題
もんだい

次の問題から、正しい答えを一つ選んでください。

1. 猿は、花火を見たことがありますか？[1]

  A.　はい、見たことがあります

  B.　いいえ、見たことがありません

2. どうして、みんなは「わくわく」しましたか？[2]

  A.　初めて、花火を見ることができるから

  B.　くじを引くことができるから

  C.　赤い蝋燭がきれいだったから

3. 誰が火を付けましたか？[3]

  A.　猿

  B.　イタチ

  C.　猪

---

[1] Q1. Has the monkey ever seen fireworks?

[2] Q2. Why was everyone "わくわく"?

[3] Q3. Who (ended up) lighting the fire?

4. どうして、みんなは、目と耳を塞ぎましたか？[4]

   A.   花火が怖かったから

   B.   目と耳が痛かったから

   C.   花火を見たくなかったから

5. この話の後に、どんな話が続くと思いますか？[5]

   A.   ドンッ

      空に、きれいな花火が上がりました。

      でも、誰も花火を見ることができませんでした。

   B.   「あれ？　どうして？」

      みんな、ゆっくり目を開けました。

      そして、あれは花火じゃないと、わかりました。

   C.   ドンッ

      花火がそこで爆発しました。

      みんな、目と耳を塞いでいましたから、大丈夫でした。

---

[4] Q4. Why did everyone cover their eyes and ears?

[5] Q5. How do you think the story will continue?

| The Red Candle   19

ANSWERS・解答
<ruby>解答<rt>かいとう</rt></ruby>

I. A.　はい、<ruby>見<rt>み</rt></ruby>たことがあります

Yes, he has seen them.

2. A.　<ruby>初<rt>はじ</rt></ruby>めて、<ruby>花火<rt>はなび</rt></ruby>を<ruby>見<rt>み</rt></ruby>ることができるから

Because they will be able to see fireworks for the first time.

3. C.　<ruby>猪<rt>いのしし</rt></ruby>

The boar

4. A.　<ruby>花火<rt>はなび</rt></ruby>が<ruby>怖<rt>こわ</rt></ruby>かったから

Because they were afraid of fireworks

5. B.　「あれ？　どうして？」
みんな、ゆっくり<ruby>目<rt>め</rt></ruby>を<ruby>開<rt>あ</rt></ruby>けました。
そして、あれは<ruby>花火<rt>はなび</rt></ruby>じゃないと、わかりました。

"Huh? Why?"

Everyone slowly opened their eyes.

Then, they realized that those were not fireworks.

THE RED CANDLE WITH ENGLISH TRANSLATION

ある日、猿が、山から村の方へ遊びに行くと、赤い蝋燭が一本ありました。

One day, a monkey came down from the mountain into the village to play. There was a single red candle.

赤い色の蝋燭を見たことがありませんでしたから、猿はその蝋燭を花火だと思いました。

The monkey had never seen a red candle before, so he thought it was a firework rocket.

猿は、赤い蝋燭を山へ持って帰りました。そして、とても大切にしました。

The monkey took it back to the mountain. He took good care of the candle.

山のみんなはびっくりしました。

Everyone in the mountain was surprised.

鹿も、猪も、ウサギも、亀も、イタチも、タヌキも、狐も、まだ一回も見たことがないからです。

The deer, the boar, the rabbit, the turtle, the weasel, the tanuki[6], and the fox had never seen anything like it before either.

「それは何？」

「ほう、きれいだね」

「これは、すごい」

"What is it?"

"Wow! It's beautiful!"

"That's awesome!"

鹿や、猪や、ウサギや、亀や、イタチや、タヌキや、狐は、押し合って赤い蝋燭を見ました。

The deer, the boar, the rabbit, the turtle, the weasel, the tanuki, and the fox pushed in to get a look at the candle.

すると猿が、「あぶない、あぶない。これは花火ですから、近づくと爆発するよ」と言いました。

---

[6] Tanuki are Japanese animals sometimes called raccoon dogs.

"Watch out, watch out! If you get close to it, it will explode!" the monkey said.

「わぁー！」みんなは、急いで遠くへ行きました。

"Ahh!" Everyone hurried to get far away.

猿は、花火がとても大きな音がして、とてもきれいに空に上がる、とみんなに教えてあげました。

The monkey told everyone that fireworks make a big noise and soar beautifully through the sky.

「花火はそんなにきれいなの？」みんなは、花火を見たいと思いました。

"Are fireworks that beautiful?" Everyone wanted to see fireworks.

「じゃあ、今晩、山の一番上で花火を打ち上げましょう」と猿が言いました。みんなはとても喜びました。そして、花火のことを思って、うっとりしました。

"How about we launch the firework on top of the mountain tonight?" the monkey said. Everyone was very happy. They were entranced thinking about the fireworks.

夜になりました。みんなは、わくわくしながら山の一番上に着きました。

It was nighttime. Everyone was excited when they reached the top of the mountain.

「さあ、花火を打ち上げましょう」でも、困ったことがありました。誰も火を付けないのです。

"Okay, let's launch this firework," but there was a problem. Nobody could light a fire.

みんな、花火を見たいのですが、火が好きではありませんでした。

Everyone wanted to see fireworks, but no one liked fire.

「これでは花火が上がりませんので、火を付ける人を、くじで決めましょう」

"We can't light the firework as things are. Let's decide who will light the fire by drawing lots."

最初は、亀になりました。

At first, it was the turtle's turn to try.

亀は、元気を出して花火の方へ行きました。

The turtle summoned up his willpower and went up to the firework.

でも亀は、花火のそばに来ると、首が出て来なくなりました。

But, when he came close to the firework, he got too scared, and his neck wouldn't leave his shell.

もう一回くじを引きました。次は、イタチです。

They drew lots again. It was the weasel's turn.

イタチは、目が悪いですから、蝋燭の周りをうろうろするだけでした。

The weasel had bad eyes, so he ended up just wandering around the candle.

それを見ていた猪は、前に出ました。

Seeing all that, the boar came forward.

猪は、勇気があります。すぐに花火のところへ行きました。そして、本当に火を付けました。

He was brave. He immediately went right up to the firework and actually lit the fire.

みんな、びっくりして隠れました。

Everyone was surprised and hid.

そして、耳を塞ぎました。

They covered their ears.

耳だけではありません。目も塞ぎました。

They didn't just cover their ears. They also covered their eyes.

「‥‥‥‥‥」

何も音がしません。蝋燭は、静かに静かに燃えているだけでした。

There was no noise. The candle just burned ever so quietly.

The Mask

マスク

エドワードは、困っていました。初めての日本旅行でしたから、道に迷ったのです。町も、もう暗い。

エドワードは、近くを歩いていた女の人に聞きました。

「すみません。道に迷ったんです。ここへ行きたいんですが……」

「あら、それは大変ですね。案内しますよ」

女の人は、エドワードと歩きながら、話しました。

「こんなときに、旅行は大変だったでしょう」

病気が世界に広まって、旅行が難しくなったのです。

「ええ、そうですね。でも、みんなマスクをしていますから。私も安心して、旅行に行くことができるんです」

「あら、マスクがあって、安心だと思っていると、怖いことになりますよ」

「どうしてですか?」

「日本には、口裂け女[7]がいるんです。おばけですよ。マスクをしているきれいな女の人ですが、マスクを取ると、口が耳まで裂けているんです」

---

[7] a kind of Japanese monster

エドワードは、笑って答えます。

「ははははは。どこでも、おばけの話はありますね。子どものときは、怖かったですが、今は大丈夫です」

それを聞くと、女の人は、笑ってマスクを取りました。

「これでも？」

女の人の口は、耳まで裂けていました。

エドワードは、びっくりして言いました。

「あなたもだったんですか！」

「え？」

エドワードもマスクを取りました。エドワードの口には、長くて鋭い歯がありました。エドワードは吸血鬼[8]だったのです。

「病気にはなりませんが、マスクがあると、安心して旅行することができますね」

「ええ、本当に」

---

[8] vampire

VOCABULARY LIST・単語リスト

- 道に迷う / *michinimayou* / to be lost, to get lost
- 案内する / *annaisuru* / to show the way, to show around, to guide
- 世界 / *sekai* / world
- 広まる / *hiromaru* / to spread
- マスク / *masuku* / mask
- 安心する / *anshinsuru* / to feel safe, to be relieved
- 口裂け女 / *kuchisakeonna* / Kuchisakeonna (a kind of Japanese monster)
- おばけ / *obake* / monster
- 裂ける / *sakeru* / to be split
- 鋭い / *surudoi* / sharp
- 歯 / *ha* / teeth
- 吸血鬼 / *kyūketsuki* / vampire

QUESTIONS・問題

次の問題から、正しい答えを一つ選んでください。

1. エドワードは、よく日本へ来ますか？[9]

　A.　はい、よく来ます

　B.　いいえ、初めてです

2. 女の人が言った「怖いこと」は、何ですか？[10]

　A.　病気になる

　B.　おばけに会う

　C.　道に迷う

3. エドワードは、おばけが怖いですか？[11]

　A.　はい、今も怖いです

　B.　いいえ、今は怖くないです

---

[9] Q1. Does Edward often visit Japan?

[10] Q2. What is the "怖いこと" the woman said?

[11] Q3. Is Edward afraid of monsters?

4. 女の人は、本当は、何でしたか？ [12]

    A. 口裂け女

    B. 吸血鬼

5. 「あなたもだったんですか！」とは、どういう意味ですか？ [13]

    A. 私も、マスクが取りたかったです

    B. 私も、本当はおばけが怖いです

    C. 私も、あなたと同じおばけです

---

[12] Q4. What was the woman, really?

[13] Q5. What does "あなたもだったんですか！" mean?

ANSWERS・解答
かいとう

---

1. B.　いいえ、初めてです
はじ

No, it's his first time.

2. B.　おばけに会う
あ

To see a monster.

3. B.　いいえ、今は怖くないです
いま　こわ

No, he isn't afraid of monsters now.

4. A.　口裂け女
くちさ　おんな

Kuchisakeonna

5. C.　私も、あなたと同じおばけです
わたし　　　　　おな

I am a monster just like you.

THE MASK WITH ENGLISH TRANSLATION

エドワードは、困っていました。

Edward was in trouble.

初めての日本旅行でしたから、道に迷ったのです。

It was his first trip to Japan, and he was lost.

町も、もう暗い。

The town he was in was dark.

エドワードは、近くを歩いていた女の人に聞きました。

Edward approached a lady walking nearby and asked,

「すみません。道に迷ったんです。ここへ行きたいんで

すが……」

"Excuse me. I'm lost. I want to get here, but…"

「あら、それは大変ですね。案内しますよ」

"Oh dear. That's rough. Let me show you the way."

女の人は、エドワードと歩きながら、話しました。

The woman walked with Edward and talked.

「こんなときに、旅行は大変だったでしょう」

"I bet it was difficult traveling at this time."

病気が世界に広まって、旅行が難しくなったのです。

A disease was spreading throughout the world, and traveling had gotten difficult.

「ええ、そうですね。でも、みんなマスクをしていますから。私も安心して、旅行に行くことができるんです」

"Yeah, that's true. But, everyone is wearing a mask. I feel safe traveling."

「あら、マスクがあって、安心だと思っていると、怖いことになりますよ」

"Oh. But, frightening things happen when you feel safe because everyone is wearing a mask."

「どうしてですか？」

"Why is that?"

「日本には、口裂け女がいるんです。おばけですよ。マスクをしているきれいな女の人ですが、マスクを取ると、口が耳まで裂けているんです」

"In Japan, we have Kuchisake Onna. They are monsters. They are beautiful when they wear a mask, but when they take it off, their mouth is split ear to ear.

エドワードは、笑って答えます。

Edward laughed and replied,

「はははは。どこにでも、おばけの話はあります

ね。子どものときは、怖かったですが、今は大丈夫で

す」

"Hahaha. Every country has stories about monsters.

When I was a kid, they used to scare me. But now I'm

okay."

それを聞くと、女の人は、笑ってマスクを取りました。

The lady heard that, laughed, and then took off her

mask.

「これでも？」

"How about this?"

女の人の口は、耳まで裂けていました。

Her mouth was split open ear to ear.

エドワードは、びっくりして言いました。

Edward was surprised and said,

「あなたもだったんですか！」

"So you're a monster too."

「え？」

What?"

エドワードもマスクを取りました。

Edward took off his mask.

エドワードの口には、長くて鋭い歯がありました。

He had long sharp teeth in his mouth.

エドワードは吸血鬼だったのです。

Edward was a vampire.

「病気にはなりませんが、マスクがあると、安心して旅行することができますね」

"I don't get sick, but I feel safe when I travel with a mask."

「ええ、本当に」

"I understand."

You Can Read Japanese!

苦手なもの
にがて

「りささんは、苦手なペットはいる？」先生は、りさに聞きました。

「あの、犬が……」

「犬が苦手なの？」

「はい、子どものときに、犬が私の手を噛んで。それから、怖くなって」

「わかったわ。じゃあ、犬がいない家がいいわね」

りさの大学では、学生はみんな、一か月間の海外留学をします。先生は、ホストファミリーのことを、りさと話していました。

りさの乗った飛行機が、オーストラリアに着きました。

「りさー！　りさー！」ホストファミリーが、空港まで来ていました。

「はい、ここにいます。りさです。今日からよろしくお願いします」

「ようこそ。オーストラリアへ」明るい笑顔でした。

「お腹は空いている？　オーストラリアの牛肉は美味しいですよ。帰って、食べましょうね」

良かった、いい人たちだ。りさは、安心しました。

車で二時間。ホストファミリーの家に着きました。

「わんわん！　わんわん！」

りさは、目を大きく開けました。

隣の家よね？　いえ、テレビの音？

「いらっしゃい」とホストのお母さんがドアを開けました。そこには、大きなゴールデンレトリバーが！

「えぇ！　ちょっと待って」

りさは、急いで外に出ました。すると、小さなトイプードルがりさの方へ走って来ました。

「二匹もいる！　きゃー！　嫌だ、来ないで」

りさは、ホストファミリーに犬が苦手なことを話しました。そして、ホストのお母さんがゆっくりと言いました。

「みんな、苦手なものはありますよね。りさの部屋は二階だから、ドアを閉めると、犬は入らないわ。

下に降りて来るときは、リードを付けますから。だから、大丈夫よ」

「……ありがとうございます」

ホストファミリーが困ると思って、犬のことを、もう言いませんでした。

それから、三週間。ある木曜日の夜でした。ホストファミリーは、レストランへ行っていました。りさは、宿題をしなければなりませんでしたから、一人で家にいました。

少し休んでいるとき、庭の方から音が聞こえました。

「もう、帰って来たの？」りさが窓から外を見ると、知らない男がいました。

泥棒？

家の前を行ったり、来たりして、中を見ています。りさは、危ないと思って、裏口の方へ行きました。

「待って。犬たちは？　犬も、大切な家族よね」

犬は苦手です。でも、泥棒が家に入って来ると、犬も危ない。

42

りさは、犬のリードを取りました。

「さあ、一緒に逃げるよ！」

裏口を開けると、二匹の犬は、泥棒のいる方へ走っ

て行きました。

「そっちじゃない！」

「わん！　わんわん！」

びっくりした泥棒は、どこかへ逃げていきました。

犬たちは、りさのところへ帰って来て、座りました。

「怖かった。ありがとう」りさは、初めて犬たちの頭を

なでました。

「あと一週間か。もっと早く友達になりたかったね」

VOCABULARY LIST・単語リスト

- 苦手/ *nigate* / to not like, to dislike, to not be good at (used as an adjective in Japanese)
- 噛む/ *kamu* / to bite
- 海外留学/ *kaigairyūgaku* / study abroad
- ホストファミリー/ *hosutofwamirī* / host family
- 空港/ *kūkō* / airport
- 笑顔/ *egao* / smile
- ゴールデンレトリバー/ *gōrudenretoribā* / golden retriever
- トイプードル/ *toipūdoru* / toy poodle
- リード/ *rīdo* / leash
- 泥棒/ *dorobō* / burglar
- 裏口/ *uraguchi* / backdoor
- 逃げる/ *nigeru* / to run away
- なでる/ *naderu* / to pet, to pat

QUESTIONS・問題

次の問題から、正しい答えを一つ選んでください。

1. りさが苦手なものは、何ですか？[14]

   A. 犬

   B. ホストファミリー

   C. 留学

2. どうして、りさは「目を大きく開けました」か？[15]

   A. 家が大きかったから

   B. 犬の声が聞こえたから

   C. 犬がかわいかったから

---

[14] Q1. What does Risa dislike?

[15] Q2. Why did Risa "目を大きく開けました"?

3. りさが一人で宿題をしているとき、誰が家に来ました

か？16

    A. ホストファミリー

    B. 犬

    C. 知らない男

4. どうして、泥棒は逃げましたか？17

    A. 犬が走ってきたから

    B. りさが大きな声を出したから

    C. ホストファミリーが帰ってきたから

5. 「あと一週間か」とは、どういう意味ですか？18

    A. 一週間、一人で家にいる

    B. 一週間後、日本へ帰る

    C. 一週間後、また泥棒が来る

---

16 Q3. Who came to the house when Risa was doing her homework alone?

17 Q4. Why did the burglar run away?

18 Q5. What does "あと一週間か" mean?

ANSWERS · 解答

1. A. 犬

Dogs

2. B. 犬の声が聞こえたから

Because she heard the dog's bark.

3. C. 知らない男

An unknown man

4. A. 犬が走ってきたから

Because the dogs ran toward the burglar.

5. B. 一週間後、日本へ帰る

A week later, she will go back to Japan.

DISLIKES WITH ENGLISH TRANSLATION

「りささんは、苦手なペットはいる？」

"Risa, is there a kind of pet you don't like?"

先生は、りさに聞きました。

The teacher asked Risa.

「あの、犬が……」

"Um, dogs…"

「犬が苦手なの？」

"You don't like dogs?

「はい、子どものときに、犬が私の手を噛んで。それから、怖くなって」

"Yes, when I was a kid, I was bit by a dog. I've been afraid of them ever since."

「わかったわ。じゃあ、犬がいない家がいいわね」

"Got it. So, a home without dogs would be good."

りさの大学では、学生はみんな、一か月間の海外留学をします。

Risa was a university student, and all the students were going to do a one-month study-abroad trip.

先生は、ホストファミリーのことを、りさと話していま
した。

Risa was talking with her teacher about a host-family.

りさの乗った飛行機が、オーストラリアに着きました。

The plane Risa was riding on arrived in Australia.

「りさー！　りさー！」

"Risa! Risa!"

ホストファミリーが、空港まで来ていました。

Her host family had come to the airport.

「はい、ここにいます。りさです。今日からよろしく
お願いします」

"Yes! I'm here. I'm Risa. Nice to meet you."

「ようこそ。オーストラリアへ」明るい笑顔でした。

"Welcome to Australia!" Her host family said with
cheerful smiles.

「お腹は空いている？　オーストラリアの牛肉は美味し
いですよ。帰って、食べましょうね」

"Are you hungry? Australian beef is delicious. Let's
eat when we get back."

良かった、いい人たちだ。

Oh, good. They seemed like good people.

りさは、安心しました。

She was relieved.

車で二時間。ホストファミリーの家に着きました。

She was in the car for two hours. She got to her host

family's house.

「わんわん！　わんわん！」

"Woof, woof! Woof, woof!"

りさは、目を大きく開けました。

Risa's eyes opened wide.

隣の家よね？　いえ、テレビの音？

Is it the neighbors? A noise on the TV?

「いらっしゃい」とホストのお母さんがドアを開けまし

た。

"Welcome!" Her host mother said and opened the door.

そこには、大きなゴールデンレトリバーが！

There was a big golden retriever waiting for her.

「えぇ！　ちょっと待って」りさは、急いで外に出ました。

"W-wait a minute!" She ran outside.

すると、小さなトイプードルがりさの方へ走って来ました。

A tiny toy poodle came running after her.

「二匹もいる！　きゃー！　嫌だ、来ないで」

"There's two of them! Ah! No! Don't come here!"

りさは、ホストファミリーに犬が苦手なことを話しました。

Risa told her host family that she disliked dogs.

そして、ホストのお母さんがゆっくりと言いました。

Her host mother told her slowly,

「みんな、苦手なものはありますよね。りさの部屋は二階だから、ドアを閉めると、犬は入らないわ。

"Everyone has things they don't like. Risa's room is on the second floor. If you close the door, the dogs won't come in.

下に降りて来るときは、リードを付けますから。だか
ら、大丈夫よ」

When you come down, I'll put a leash on them. So,
don't worry about it."

「……ありがとうございます」

"... Thank you very much."

ホストファミリーが困ると思って、犬のことを、も
う言いませんでした。

She didn't want to bother her host family, so she didn't
say anything more about the dogs.

それから、三週間。ある木曜日の夜でした。

Three weeks later. It was a Thursday evening.

ホストファミリーは、レストランへ行っていました。

Her host family had gone to a restaurant.

りさは、宿題をしなければなりませんでしたから、
一人で家にいました。

Risa had to do her homework, so she was home alone.

少し休んでいるとき、庭の方から音が聞こえました。

While she was taking a break, she heard a noise from the yard.

「もう、帰って来たの？」

"Did they already come back?"

りさが窓から外を見ると、知らない男がいました。

Risa looked out the window. There was a man she didn't recognize.

泥棒？

Is that a burglar?

家の前を行ったり、来たりして、中を見ています。

He was going back and forth in the front of the house, checking inside.

りさは、危ないと思って、裏口の方へ行きました。

Risa was afraid and went to the backdoor.

「待って。犬たちは？ 犬も、大切な家族よね」

"Wait. The dogs? The dogs are also a precious part of the family."

犬は苦手です。でも、泥棒が家に入って来る
と、犬も危ない。

She didn't like dogs. But, if a burglar came in, the dogs
would be in danger.

りさは、犬のリードを取りました。

Risa took the dogs by the leash.

「さあ、一緒に逃げるよ！」

"Okay, let's get out of here!"

裏口を開けると、二匹の犬は、泥棒のいる方へ走っ
て行きました。

She opened the back door, and the two dogs ran
toward the burglar.

「そっちじゃない！」

"Not that way!"

「わん！　わんわん！」

"Woof! Woof, woof!"

びっくりした泥棒は、どこかへ逃げていきました。

The surprised burglar ran away.

犬たちは、りさのところへ帰って来て、座りました。

The dogs came back to Risa and sat.

「怖かった。ありがとう」

"That was scary. Thank you!'

りさは、初めて犬たちの頭をなでました。

Risa patted the dogs' heads for the first time.

「あと一週間か。もっと早く友達になりたかったね」

"Only one week left. I wish we had become friends

sooner."

You Can Read Japanese!

A Certain Medicine

ある薬
くすり

夜の二時ごろ。国の研究所の前に、二人の泥棒がいました。

泥棒は、研究所のドアにパソコンを繋ぎました。

ピッピッピッ

すると、すぐにドアの鍵が開きました。

泥棒が言いました。

「お前、前より仕事が早くなったな」

「やっぱり国は、ばかだな。こんな鍵、俺たちには簡単さ」

二人は、笑いました。そして、研究所に入っていきました。

「これがその薬だ。この薬を飲むと、不老不死になる」

泥棒たちの間では、有名な薬でした。でも、誰も盗んだことはありませんでした。

二人はすぐにその薬を飲みました。

ゴクリ

「全部盗んで、早く売りたいな。これで俺たちは、大金持ちだ」

「……あれ？　なんだか頭が熱い。お前、大丈夫か？」

「ああ、力が出てくる」

「……――それは良かったです」

と、研究所の男が、話します。泥棒二人は、頭を下げて言いました。

「いい薬をありがとうございます。これからは、いいことをたくさんします」

「はい。気をつけて」

研究所から、明るい顔の二人が出ていきました。

男は、電話で話しました。

「はい、実験は上手くいきました。あの薬は、泥棒にもよく効きました」

VOCABULARY LIST・単語リスト

- 研究所 / *kenkyūjo* / (research) laboratory
- 泥棒 / *dorobō* / burglar
- パソコン / *pasokon* / laptop
- 繋ぐ / *tsunagu* / to connect
- 鍵 / *kagi* / lock, key
- 不老不死 / *furōfushi* / immortality
- 盗む / *nusumu* / to steal
- 大金持ち / *ōganemochi* / super rich
- 力 / *chikara* / strength, power
- 頭を下げる / *atamaosageru* / to hang one's head
- 気をつけて / *kiotsukete* / be careful
- 実験 / *jikken* / experiment
- 効く / *kiku* / to work, to be effective

QUESTIONS・問題

次の問題から、正しい答えを一つ選んでください。

1. 泥棒たちは、ドアに何を繋ぎましたか？[19]

A. 鍵

B. パソコン

C. 車

2. 泥棒は、「薬」をどんな薬だと思っていましたか？[20]

A. 不老不死になる薬

B. 力が出る薬

C. お金持ちになる薬

---

[19] Q1. What did the burglars connect to the door?

[20] Q2. What kind of medicine did the burglar think "薬" was?

3. 「薬」は、本当はどんな薬でしたか？[21]

    A.　不老不死になる薬

    B.　力が出る薬

    C.　悪い人をいい人に変える薬

4.　この後、二人の泥棒は、どんなことをすると思いますか？[22]

    A.　薬を売る

    B.　また、泥棒をする

    C.　いいことをする

5. お話の内容と合っているものは、どれですか？[23]

    A.　この薬は、国が作ったものだ

    B.　二人の泥棒は、今日初めて会った

    C.　二人の泥棒は、死なない

---

[21] Q3. What was the "薬" really like?

[22] Q4. What do you think the two burglars will do after this story?

[23] Q5. Which one best matches the details of the story?

ANSWERS・解答
（かいとう）

---

1. B. パソコン
（ぱ そ こ ん）

The laptop.

2. A. 不老不死になる薬
（ふ ろ う ふ し）　　（くすり）

The medicine that makes them immortal.

3. C. 悪い人をいい人に変える薬
（わる）（ひと）　（ひと）（か）（くすり）

The medicine that turns bad people into good people

4. C. いいことをする

They will do good things.

5. A. この薬は、国が作ったものだ
（くすり）　（くに）（つく）

This medicine was made by the government.

A CERTAIN MEDICINE WITH ENGLISH TRANSLATION

夜の二時ごろ。国の研究所の前に、二人の泥棒がいました。

It was two o'clock at night. Two burglars stood in front of a national research laboratory.

泥棒は、研究所のドアにパソコンを繋ぎました。

They connected a laptop to the laboratory door.

ピッピッピッ

The door went, "beep, beep, beep!"

すると、すぐにドアの鍵が開きました。

and the door's lock opened right after.

泥棒が言いました。

The burglar said,

「お前、前より仕事が早くなったな」

"You've gotten faster than before!!"

「やっぱり国は、ばかだな。こんな鍵、俺たちには簡単さ」

"This country is really stupid. We were easily able to open this lock."

二人は、笑いました。そして、研究所に入っていきました。

The two of them laughed before going inside the laboratory.

「これがその薬だ。この薬を飲むと、不老不死になる」

"This is the medicine. If we take this medicine, we will become immortal."

泥棒たちの間では、有名な薬でした。でも、誰も盗んだことはありませんでした。

There was a drug that was famous among burglars. But, nobody had ever stolen it before.

二人はすぐにその薬を飲みました。

The two of them drank the medicine right away.

ゴクリ

Gulp.

「全部盗んで、早く売りたいな。これで俺たちは、大金持ちだ」

"I want to steal it and sell it all! We're going to get super rich!"

「……あれ？　なんだか頭が熱い。お前、大丈夫か？」

"What's this? My head's getting warm. Are you good?"

「ああ、力が出てくる」

"I feel stronger."

「……──それは良かったです」

"...That's good."

と、研究所の男が、話します。泥棒二人は、頭を下げて言いました。

A man in the laboratory said. The two burglars hung their head in shame and said,

「いい薬をありがとうございます。これからは、いいことをたくさんします」

"Thank you for the good medicine. We're going to do a lot of good things."

「はい。気をつけて」

"Yes, be careful.

研究所から、明るい顔の二人が出ていきました。

The two of them left the laboratory looking cheerful.

男は、電話で話しました。

The man was speaking on the phone.

「はい、実験は上手くいきました。あの薬は、泥棒にも

よく効きました」

"Yes, the experiment went well. The medicine worked

well even on the burglars."

The Friendship Bracelet

ミサンガ

麻里子は、いつも手首にミサンガを付けています。
麻里子の大好きなミサンガです。

　このミサンガは、五年前、みかちゃんからもらいました。みかちゃんは、十歳年上のお姉さん[24]です。
麻里子の家の近くに住んでいました。

　麻里子は、みかちゃんが大好きでした。でも、五年前、
みかちゃんは、引っ越しをしました。春から、
大学へ行くのです。

「行かないで」

麻里子が悲しくて、泣いています。

「また、会うことができるから。そんなに泣かないで」

みかちゃんは、笑って言いました。

「これ、私が作ったのよ」

みかちゃんは、麻里子にきれいな色のミサンガを見せました。

「ミサンガはね、手に付けるときに、一つお願いごとを
するといいんだよ」

---

[24] older girl (literally older sister. Used to suggest a friendly relationship with the older girl.

そう言って、みかちゃんは、麻里子の手首に
ミサンガを付けました。

「ミサンガが切れたとき、お願いごとが叶うのよ。だか
ら、切れるまで大切に付けていてね」

麻里子は泣きながら、お願いごとをしました……。

麻里子は、新しい制服を着ていました。今日から、
中学生になるのです。

ぽとっ

何かが落ちる音が聞こえました。

下を見ると、ミサンガが落ちていました。

「え、どうして切れるの？　好きだったのに」

麻里子は、ミサンガをポケットに入れました。

学校へ行くバスの中。

ミサンガに、何をお願いしたかな？　思い出すことがで
きません。

みかちゃん、元気かな？　あのとき、どんなお願いごと
をしたんだっけ？

学校に着いて、教室に入りました。

ガラッ

教室のドアが開いて、先生が入って来ました。それは、先生になったみかちゃんでした。

「このクラスの担任になりました。田中みかです」

そのとき、思い出しました。

お願いごとは

「みかちゃんに、また会いたい」でした。

「本当に叶ったんだ」

みかちゃんが、麻里子を見て笑いました。

VOCABULARY LIST · 単語リスト

- 年上 / *toshiue* / older (person)
- お姉さん / *onēsan* / older girl (literally older sister. Used to suggest a friendly relationship with the older girl. It can be used with older women as well.)
- 引っ越し / *hikkoshi* / move, moving house
- お願いごと / *onegaigoto* / wish
- 手首 / *tekubi* / wrist
- 切れる / *kireru* / to break
- 叶う / *kanau* / to come true (of a wish)
- 制服 / *seifuku* / uniform
- 中学生 / *chūgakusei* / junior high school student
- 思い出す / *omoidasu* / to remember
- 担任 / *tannin* / homeroom teacher

QUESTIONS・問題

次の問題から、正しい答えを一つ選んでください。

1. 麻里子は、ミサンガをどこに付けていますか？[25]

    A. 手首

    B. 足

    C. 首

2. ミサンガは、誰が、誰にあげましたか？[26]

    A. 麻里子がみかちゃんにあげた

    B. みかちゃんが麻里子にあげた

3. どうして、麻里子は「泣いています」か？[27]

    A. みかちゃんが遠くへ行くから

    B. みかちゃんが大学へ行くから

    C. ミサンガが切れたから

---

[25] Q1. Where does Mariko wear her friendship bracelet?

[26] Q2. Who gave the friendship bracelet to whom?

[27] Q3. Why did Mariko "泣いています"?

4. 麻里子は、ミサンガに、どんな「願いごと」をしましたか？ 28

   A.　みかちゃんに、先生になってほしい

   B.　みかちゃんに、また会いたい

   C.　みかちゃんに、引っ越しをしてほしくない

5. 麻里子は、みかちゃんのことも、お願いごとも忘れていましたか？ 29

   A.　はい、どちらも忘れていました

   B.　いいえ、みかちゃんのことは忘れていませんでしたが、お願いごとは忘れていました

   C.　いいえ、みかちゃんのことは忘れていましたが、お願いごとは忘れていませんでした

---

28 Q4. What kind of "願いごと" did Mariko make on her friendship bracelet?

29 Q5. Did Mariko forget about Mika-chan and her wish?

ANSWERS・解答

---

1. A.　手首

Wrist.

2. B.　みかちゃんが麻里子にあげた

Mika-chan gave it to Mariko.

3. A.　みかちゃんが遠くへ行くから

Because Mika is going far away.

4. B.　みかちゃんに、また会いたい

She wants to see Mika-chan again.

5. B.　いいえ、みかちゃんのことは忘れていませんでした が、お願いごとは忘れていました

No, she had not forgotten about Mika-chan, but she had forgotten about her wish.

THE FRIENDSHIP BRACELET WITH ENGLISH TRANSLATION

麻里子は、いつも手首にミサンガを付けています。

Mariko always wears a friendship bracelet on her wrist.

麻里子の大好きなミサンガです。

It's Mariko's favorite bracelet.

このミサンガは、五年前、みかちゃんからもらいました。

She had gotten the bracelet from Mika-chan five years ago.

みかちゃんは、十歳年上のお姉さんです。

Mika-chan was a girl who was 10 years older than her.

麻里子の家の近くに住んでいました。

She had lived in a home near Mariko.

麻里子は、みかちゃんが大好きでした。

Mariko loved Mika-chan.

でも、五年前、みかちゃんは、引っ越しをしました。

But, Mika-chan had moved five years ago.

春から、大学へ行くのです。

Mika-chan was going to go to the university in spring.

「行かないで」麻里子が悲しくて、泣いています。

"Don't leave!" Mariko was sad and cried.

「また、会うことができるから。そんなに泣かないで」

"We'll see each other again. Don't cry."

みかちゃんは、笑って言いました。

Mika-chan said as she smiled.

「これ、私が作ったのよ」

"I made this for you."

みかちゃんは、麻里子にきれいな色のミサンガを見せました。

Mika-chan showed Mariko a friendship bracelet with beautiful colors.

「ミサンガはね、手に付けるときに、一つお願いごとをするといいんだよ」

"When you put a friendship bracelet on your wrist, you should make a wish."

そう言って、みかちゃんは、麻里子の手首に
ミサンガを付けました。

She said and put the bracelet on Mariko's wrist.

「ミサンガが切れたとき、お願いごとが叶うのよ。だか
ら、切れるまで大切に付けていてね」

"When the friendship bracelet falls apart, the wish will

come true. Take care of it until it falls apart."

麻里子は泣きながら、お願いごとをしました……。

Mariko cried as she made a wish.

麻里子は、新しい制服を着ていました。

Mariko was wearing her new uniform.

今日から、中学生になるのです。

She was a junior high school student as of today.

ぽとっ

Plop.

何かが落ちる音が聞こえました。

She heard the noise of something falling.

下を見ると、ミサンガが落ちていました。

She looked down to see her friendship bracelet on the ground.

「え、どうして切れるの？　好きだったのに」

"What? Why did it break? I really liked it."

麻里子は、ミサンガをポケットに入れました。

Mariko put the friendship bracelet in her pocket.

学校へ行くバスの中。

She was on the bus going to school.

ミサンガに、何をお願いしたかな？

What did she wish on the friendship bracelet?

思い出すことができません。

She couldn't remember.

みかちゃん、元気かな？

How was Mika-chan doing?

あのとき、どんなお願いごとをしたんだっけ？

What did I wish for at that time?

学校に着いて、教室に入りました。

When she got to school, she went into the classroom.

ガラッ

Click.

教室のドアが開いて、先生が入って来ました。

The classroom door opened and the teacher walked in.

それは、先生になったみかちゃんでした。

Standing there was Mika-chan, who had become a teacher.

「このクラスの担任になりました。田中みかです」

"I'm this class's homeroom teacher, Tanaka Mika."

そのとき、思い出しました。

Then, she remembered.

お願いごとは「みかちゃんに、また会いたい」でした。

Her wish was, "I want to see Mika-chan again."

「本当に叶ったんだ」

"It really came true."

みかちゃんが、麻里子を見て笑いました。

Mika-chan looked at Mariko and laughed.

Japanese Cuisine

日本の料理

クラークさんは、仕事で日本に来ています。会社の昼休みに、同僚がクラークさんに聞きました。

「やあ、日本はどうだい?」

「ああ、いいところだね、日本は」

「それは良かった。日本を好きになってもらうと、私も嬉しいよ」

「とても好きになったよ。一番は和食だね。ヘルシーでおいしい。今朝も白いご飯と、みそ汁と、焼き魚を食べたんだ」

「本当に和食が好きなんだね。じゃあ、昼も和食がいいかい?」

「いや、今日は和食じゃないものがいいな。レストランに行かないか?」

そう言って、二人は、近くのレストランに行きました。

「私は、コーヒーとベーグル。あ、ドーナツもあるね。それも一つ」

「僕も同じものを」

料理が来て、二人は食べ始めました。すると、すぐにクラークさんの手が止まりました。

「ん？　初めて食べる味だな。どうやって作ったのかな？」

レストランの人に聞くと、

「ご飯を使ったベーグルと、豆腐を使ったドーナツです」と答えました。

クラークさんは、苦笑いしました。

「和食じゃない昼ご飯が良かったんだけど、これは洋食かな？　和食かな？」

同僚は笑って、答えました。

「和食でも、洋食でもいいんじゃないかな。そうだ、知ってる？　日本では計画が上手くいかなかったときに、こう言うんだ」

同僚は、ベーグルとドーナツを持って、言いました。

「計画に穴があった」

VOCABULARY LIST・単語リスト

- 同僚 / *dōryō* / coworker
- 和食 / *washoku* / Japanese food
- ヘルシー / *herushī* / healthy
- みそ汁 / *misoshiru* / miso soup
- 焼き魚 / *yakizakana* / grilled fish
- ベーグル / *bēguru* / bagel
- ドーナツ / *dōnatsu* / donut
- 味 / *aji* / flavor, taste
- 豆腐 / *tōfu* / tofu
- 苦笑いする / *nigawaraisuru* / to laugh ironically or bitterly, to force laughter, to force a smile[30]
- 洋食 / *yōshoku* / Western food
- 計画 / *keikaku* / plan
- 穴 / *ana* / hole

---

[30] It's difficult to translate this in English but it's a common phenomenon in Japan. You don't actually think something is funny or worth smiling at, but you laugh and smile anyway out of disgust or mockery.

QUESTIONS・問題

次の問題から、正しい答えを一つ選んでください。

1. 同僚は、レストランで何を食べましたか？[31]

    A. 和食

    B. ベーグルとコーヒー

    C. ベーグルとコーヒーとドーナツ

2. どうして、クラークさんの「手が止まりました」か？[32]

    A. 料理がおいしくなかったから

    B. いつも食べているものと味が同じではなかったから

    C. 本当は和食が食べたかったから

---

[31] Q1. What did the coworker eat at the restaurant?

[32] Q2. Why did Mr. Clarke's "手が止まりました"?

3. このレストランのベーグルとドーナツは、洋食です
か？　和食ですか？33

A.　洋食

B.　和食

C.　どちらかわからない

4. どうして、同僚は「計画に穴があった」と言いました
か？34

A.　クラークさんは、食べたかったものを、食べるこ
とができなかったから

B.　クラークさんは、和食を食べたかったが、食べる
ことができなかったから

C.　仕事が上手くいっていないから

5. お話の内容と<u>合っていない</u>ものは、どれですか？35

A.　クラークさんは、ヘルシーな料理が好きだ

B.　クラークさんは、日本で働いている

C.　クラークさんは、前からずっと日本に住んでいる

---

33 Q3. Are the bagels and donuts at this restaurant Western food or Japanese food?

34 Q4. Why did the coworker say "計画に穴があった"?

35 Q5. Which one does NOT match the details of the story?

ANSWERS・解答
<ruby>解答<rt>かいとう</rt></ruby>

1. C.　ベーグルとコーヒーとドーナツ

Bagels, coffee, and donuts.

2. B.　いつも食べているものと味が同じではなかったか
ら

Because it didn't taste the same as what he usually
eats.

3. C.　どちらかわからない

Neither. / It's unclear which it is.

4. A.　クラークさんは、食べたかったものを、食べるこ
とができなかったから

Because Mr. Clark could not eat what he wanted to
eat.

5. C.　クラークさんは、前からずっと日本に住んでいる

Mr. Clark has been living in Japan for a long time.

JAPANESE CUISINE WITH ENGLISH TRANSLATION

クラークさんは、仕事で日本に来ています。

Mr. Clarke had come to Japan for work.

会社の昼休みに、同僚がクラークさんに聞きました。

On his company's lunch break, a coworker asked Mr. Clarke,

「やあ、日本はどうだい？」

"Hey, how's Japan?"

「ああ、いいところだね、日本は」

"Yeah! It's really nice!"

「それは良かった。日本を好きになってもらうと、私も嬉しいよ」

"That's good! I'm glad you like Japan!"

「とても好きになったよ。一番は和食だね。ヘルシーでおいしい。今朝も白いご飯と、みそ汁と、焼き魚を食べたんだ」

90

"I really love it. I like Japanese food the best. It's healthy and delicious. I ate white rice, miso soup, and grilled fish for breakfast."

「本当に和食が好きなんだね。じゃあ、昼も和食がいいかい？」

"You really like Japanese food, huh. So, is Japanese food good for lunch?"

「いや、今日は和食じゃないものがいいな。レストランに行かないか？」

"No. I want something not Japanese for lunch today. Let's go to a restaurant."

そう言って、二人は、近くのレストランに行きました。

He said and the two of them went to a nearby restaurant.

「私は、コーヒーとベーグル。あ、ドーナツもあるね。それも一つ」

"I'll have a coffee and a bagel. Oh, there are donuts too. One of those as well."

「僕も同じものを」

"I'll have the same."

料理が来て、二人は食べ始めました。

The food came out and the two of them started eating.

すると、すぐにクラークさんの手が止まりました。

Mr. Clarke put his hands down.

「ん？　初めて食べる味だな。どうやって作ったのか

な？」

"Hmm? I haven't eaten this before. How did they make

this?"

レストランの人に聞くと、

「ご飯を使ったベーグルと、豆腐を使ったドーナツで

す」と答えました。

He asked someone at the restaurant and they replied,

"the bagel was made with rice and the donut was made

with tofu."

クラークさんは、苦笑いしました。

Mr. Clarke laughed ironically.

「和食じゃない昼ご飯が良かったんだけど、これは洋食かな？　和食かな？」

"I wanted some non-Japanese food for lunch. Is this western food? Is it Japanese food?"

同僚は笑って、答えました。

His coworker laughed.

「和食でも、洋食でもいいんじゃないかな。そうだ、知ってる？　日本では計画が上手くいかなかったときに、こう言うんだ」

"Does it matter if it's Japanese or western food? Hey, do you know what Japanese people say when a plan doesn't go well?"

同僚は、ベーグルとドーナツを持って、言いました。

The coworker took the bagel and donut in hand and said,

「計画に穴があった」

"There was a hole in the plan."

Candy

飴（あめ）だま

春のあたたかい日。小さな子どもを二人連れ
た女の人が、渡し舟に乗りました。
舟が出るとき、

「おおい、ちょっとまってくれ」
向こうから、さむらいが走ってきて、舟に乗りました。
黒いひげがあって、大きな体の、おさむらいさん。
今日は、ぽかぽかあたたかいです。

こっくりこっくり
さむらいは眠りました。

こっくりこっくり
子どもたちは、それが面白くて、ふふふ、と笑いまし
た。
お母さんは、子どもたちに言いました。
「静かにしなさい」
さむらいが怒ると思ったからです。
一人の子どもが
「お母さん、飴だまちょうだい」と手を出しました。
すると、お姉さんも、
「お母さん、あたしにも」と言いました。

お母さんが袋の中を見ると、飴だまは一つだけでした。

「あたしにちょうだい」

「あたしにちょうだい」

飴だまは一つだけでしたから、お母さんは、困りました。

「いい子たちだから待っててね。向こうの町で買ってあげるからね」

「ちょうだいよお」

「ちょうだいよお」

眠っていたさむらいは、ぱっちりと目を開けて、子どもたちを見ていました。

「静かにして、ね」お母さんは、子どもたちに言いました。でも、子どもたちは、まだ言っています。

すると、さむらいが刀を抜いて、お母さんと子どもたちの前にやってきました。

お母さんは、真っ青になって、子どもたちの前に立ちました。さむらいが子どもたちを殺すと思ったのです。

「飴だまを出せ」

と、さむらいは、言いました。

お母さんは、とても怖かったですが、飴だまを出しまし
た。

さむらいは、それを刀で二つに切りました。

そして、それを二人の子どもにやりました。

それから、またこっくりこっくり、眠りはじめました。

VOCABULARY LIST · 単語リスト

- 渡し舟 / *watashibune* / ferry
- 向こう / *mukō* / across the way
- さむらい / *samurai* / samurai
- こっくり / *kokkuri* / this is an onomatopoeia that sounds like nodding and dozing off
- 眠る / *nemuru* / to fall asleep
- 飴だま / *amedama* / candy
- ちょうだい / *chōdai* / give me please
- 袋 / *fukuro* / bag
- ぱっちり / *pattchiri* / this is an onomatopoeia that sounds when one's eyes burst open
- 刀 / *katana* / Japanese sword
- 抜く / *nuku* / to drew out
- 真っ青 / *massao* / pale
- 殺す / *korosu* / to kill

QUESTIONS・問題

次の問題から、正しい答えを一つ選んでください。

1. どうして、子どもたちは「ふふふ、と笑いました」か？ [36]

   A.　眠っているさむらいが、面白かったから

   B.　怒ったさむらいが、面白かったから

   C.　走ってくるさむらいが、面白かったから

2. どうして、さむらいは起きましたか？ [37]

   A.　子どもがうるさかったから

   B.　飴だまが食べたかったから

   C.　もうすぐ町に着くから

---

[36] Q1. Why did the children "ふふふ、と笑いました"?

[37] Q2. Why did the samurai wake up?

3. どうして、お母さんは、「真っ青」になりました
か？ 38
   A. さむらいが、飴だまを取ると思ったから
   B. さむらいが、飴だまを切ると思ったから
   C. さむらいが、子どもたちを切ると思ったから

4. どうして、さむらいは、飴だまを切りましたか？ 39
   A. もっと寝たかったから
   B. 子どもが嫌いだったから
   C. 早く町へ行きたかったから

5. この後、誰が飴だまを食べましたか？ 40
   A. さむらい
   B. 子ども二人
   C. 子ども一人

---

38 Q3. Why was the mother "真っ青"?

39 Q4. Why did the samurai cut the candy in half?

40 Q5. Who ate the candy after this story?

ANSWERS・解答
<small>かいとう</small>

---

1. A. 眠っているさむらいが、面白かったから
<small>ねむ</small> <small>おもしろ</small>

Because the sleeping samurai was funny.

2. A. 子どもがうるさかったから
<small>こ</small>

Because the children were noisy.

3. C. さむらいが、子どもたちを切ると思ったから
<small>こ</small> <small>き</small> <small>おも</small>

Because she thought the samurai would cut her children's heads with his sword.

4. A. もっと寝たかったから
<small>ね</small>

Because he wanted to sleep more.

5. B. 子ども二人
<small>こ</small> <small>ふたり</small>

The two children.

CANDY WITH ENGLISH TRANSLATION

春のあたたかい日。小さな子どもを二人連れ
た女の人が、渡し舟に乗りました。

It was a warm spring day. A woman with two children
was riding a ferry.

舟が出るとき、「おおい、ちょっとま ってくれ」
向こうから、さむらいが走ってきて、舟に乗りました。

When the ferry took off, a samurai came running from
across the way onto the ferry, yelling, "Hey, wait!"

黒いひげがあって、大きな体の、おさむらいさん。

He was a samurai with a black beard and a large body.

今日は、ぽかぽかあたたかいです。

Today was a balmy spring day.

こっくりこっくり

He started to doze off.

さむらいは眠りました。

The samurai fell asleep.

こっくりこっくり

He nodded and dozed off.

子どもたちは、それが面白くて、ふふふ、と笑いまし

た。

The children thought it was funny and laughed,

"hehehe."

お母さんは、子どもたちに言いました。

「静かにしなさい」

The mom told the children, "be quiet!"

さむらいが怒ると思ったからです。

She thought the samurai would get angry.

一人の子どもが

「お母さん、飴だまちょうだい」と手を出しました。

One child said, "Mommy, candy please!" and held out

her hand.

すると、お姉さんも、

「お母さん、あたしにも」と言いました。

Her older sister also "Mom, me too!" she said.

お母さんが袋の中を見ると、飴だまは一つだけでした。

Her mom looked in her bag. There was only one candy.

「あたしにちょうだい」「あたしにちょうだい」

"Give it to me!" "Give it to me!"

飴だまは一つだけでしたから、お母さんは、困りました。

There was only one candy, so the mother was in trouble.

「いい子たちだから待っててね。向こうの町で買ってあげるからね」

"Be a good girl and wait. I'll buy you some candy in the town on the other side."

「ちょうだいよお」「ちょうだいよお」

"Please!" "Please!"

眠っていたさむらいは、ぱっちりと目を開けて、子どもたちを見ていました。

The sleeping samurai's eyes burst open wide. He was looking at the children.

「静かにして、ね」お母さんは、子どもたちに言いました。

"Be quiet, okay?" the mother told the children.

でも、子どもたちは、まだ言っています。

But the children kept talking.

すると、さむらいが刀を抜いて、お母さんと子どもたちの前にやってきました。

The samurai drew his sword and went in front of the mother and the children.

お母さんは、真っ青になって、子どもたちの前に立ちました。さむらいが子どもたちを殺すと思ったのです。

The mother was pale, and she stood in front of the children. She thought the samurai was going to kill her children.

「飴だまを出せ」と、さむらいは、言いました。

"Give me the candy!" The samurai said.

お母さんは、とても怖かったですが、飴だまを出しました。

The mother was afraid but gave him the candy.

さむらいは、それを刀で二つに切りました。

The samurai cut it in half with a sword.

そして、それを二人の子どもにやりました。

He gave it to the two children.

それから、またこっくりこっくり、眠りはじめました。

He dozed off again and began to sleep.

Hobby

趣味

安田さんは、六十四歳。もうすぐ定年退職をします。

でも、一つ心配なことがありました。安田さんは、今まで仕事だけをしていました。結婚もしていません。あまり大きな休みもありませんでした。

これから、どう暮らすといいのでしょうか。それがわかりません。

たくさんの趣味を持っている友達に聞きました。

「私は趣味を全然持っていなくてね。今、探しているんだ。何かいい趣味を教えてほしい」

友達は、いろいろな趣味を提案しました。

「アウトドアはどうかな？　山や森へ行って、キャンプをしたり、川で遊んだりするんだ」

「虫が好きじゃないんだよ」

「じゃあ、スポーツはどう？　運動はいいよ。テニス、卓球、野球、いろいろなスポーツがあるからね。テレビで見てもいい」

「私は、もう若くない。運動は疲れるし、よく知らないスポーツは面白くない」

「じゃあ、音楽は？　ギターやピアノを教えてもらうと
いい。好きな歌を自分で弾くんだ。楽しいと思わな
い？」

「車を運転しているときや、仕事しているときに、
音楽を聴くよ。でも、ラジオで十分だ。弾きたいと
は思わないなあ」

「じゃあ、料理だ。料理を作ったり、食べたり。おいし
い料理とお酒があると、毎日が楽しくなるよ」

「料理は、お腹がいっぱいになるだけで十分だ。
お酒も好きじゃない」

いろいろな提案がありましたが、安田さんは、
全部気に入りませんでした。

そんな安田さんを見て、友達が言いました。

「君の趣味がわかったよ」

「え？　それは何？」

「君の趣味は、趣味を探すことだ」

VOCABULARY LIST · 単語リスト
_{たんごりすと}

- 定年退職 / *teinentaishoku* / retirement age[41]
- 趣味 / *shumi* / hobby
- 探す / *sagasu* / to search for
- 提案する / *teiansuru* / to propose
- アウトドア / *autodoa* / outdoor
- キャンプ / *kyampu* / camp
- 虫 / *mushi* / bug, insect
- スポーツ / *supōtsu* / sports
- 運動 / *undō* / exercise
- テニス / *tenisu* / tennis
- 卓球 / *takkyū* / table tennis
- 野球 / *yakyū* / baseball
- 音楽 / *ongaku* / music
- ギター / *gitā* / guitar
- ピアノ / *piano* / piano

---

[41] 定年 = the mandatory year for retirement and 退職 means retirement from one's job

- 弾<ruby>弾<rt>ひ</rt></ruby>く / *hiku* / to play[42]
- <ruby>十分<rt>じゅうぶん</rt></ruby> / *jūbun* / enough
- <ruby>気<rt>き</rt></ruby>に<ruby>入<rt>い</rt></ruby>る / *kiniiru* / to like

---

[42] To play an instrument. Specifically one with strings. Pianos have strings on the inside and are therefore included.

QUESTIONS・問題
<ruby>問題<rt>もんだい</rt></ruby>

<ruby>次<rt>つぎ</rt></ruby>の<ruby>問題<rt>もんだい</rt></ruby>から、<ruby>正<rt>ただ</rt></ruby>しい<ruby>答<rt>こた</rt></ruby>えを<ruby>一<rt>ひと</rt></ruby>つ<ruby>選<rt>えら</rt></ruby>んでください。

1. <ruby>安田<rt>やすだ</rt></ruby>さんの<ruby>趣味<rt>しゅみ</rt></ruby>は、<ruby>何<rt>なん</rt></ruby>ですか？ [43]

   A. <ruby>アウトドア<rt>あうとどあ</rt></ruby>

   B. <ruby>運動<rt>うんどう</rt></ruby>

   C. ない

2. <ruby>安田<rt>やすだ</rt></ruby>さんは、<ruby>奥<rt>おく</rt></ruby>さんがいますか？ [44]

   A. はい、います

   B. いいえ、いません

3. <ruby>安田<rt>やすだ</rt></ruby>さんが<ruby>嫌<rt>きら</rt></ruby>いなものは、<ruby>何<rt>なん</rt></ruby>ですか？ [45]

   A. <ruby>仕事<rt>しごと</rt></ruby>

   B. <ruby>虫<rt>むし</rt></ruby>

   C. <ruby>ピアノ<rt>ぴあの</rt></ruby>

---

[43] Q1. What is Mr. Yasuda's hobby?

[44] Q2. Does Mr. Yasuda have a wife?

[45] Q3. What does Mr. Yasuda dislike?

4. 安田さんは、車を運転するとき、何をしますか？[46]

   A. ラジオで音楽を聴く

   B. ギターを教える

   C. 仕事をする

5. お話の内容と合っているものは、どれですか？[47]

   A. 安田さんは、今、仕事をしていない

   B. 友達は、趣味がたくさんある

   C. 安田さんは、あまりご飯を食べない

---

[46] Q4. What does Mr. Yasuda do when he drives a car?

[47] Q5. Which one best matches the details of the story?

ANSWERS · 解答
<ruby>解答<rt>かいとう</rt></ruby>

I. C.　ない

Nothing.

2. B.　いいえ、いません

No, he doesn't.

3. B.　虫
<ruby>虫<rt>むし</rt></ruby>

Bugs.

4. A.　ラジオで音楽を聴く

Listening to music on the radio.

5. B.　友達は、趣味がたくさんある

His friend has lots of hobbies.

HOBBY WITH ENGLISH TRANSLATION

安田さんは、六十四歳。もうすぐ定年退職をします。

Mr. Yasuda was 64 years old. It was almost his retirement age.

でも、一つ心配なことがありました。

But, he had one worry.

安田さんは、今まで仕事だけをしていました。結婚もしていません。あまり大きな休みもありませんでした。

Mr. Yasuda had worked all his life. He wasn't married. He didn't have any big vacations either.

これから、どう暮らすといいのでしょうか。それがわかりません。

He wasn't sure how to live from here on out.

たくさんの趣味を持っている友達に聞きました。

He asked his friend who had a lot of hobbies.

「私は趣味を全然持っていなくてね。

I don't have any hobbies.

今、探しているんだ。何かいい趣味を教えてほしい」

I'm looking for one now. Tell me a good hobby."

友達は、いろいろな趣味を提案しました。

His friend proposed a few hobbies.

「アウトドアはどうかな？　山や森へ行って、キャンプをしたり、川で遊んだりするんだ」

"How about something outdoors? You can go to the mountains or the forest and camp and play in the river."

「虫が好きじゃないんだよ」

"I don't like bugs."

「じゃあ、スポーツはどう？　運動はいいよ。テニス、卓球、野球、いろいろなスポーツがあるからね。テレビで見てもいい」

"How about sports? Exercise is good for you. Tennis, ping pong, baseball. There are plenty of sports. You could even just watch them on TV."

「私は、もう若くない。運動は疲れるし、よく知らないスポーツは面白くない」

"I'm not young any more. Exercise makes me tired. Sports that I don't know well don't interest me."

「じゃあ、音楽は？　ギターやピアノを教えてもらうといい。好きな歌を自分で弾くんだ。楽しいと思わない？」

"How about music? You should have someone teach you guitar or piano. You can play your favorite songs yourself. Doesn't that sound fun?

「車を運転しているときや、仕事しているときに、音楽を聴くよ。でも、ラジオで十分だ。弾きたいとは思わないなあ」

"When I'm driving and working, I listen to music. But, the radio alone is enough for me. I don't want to play it myself."

「じゃあ、料理だ。料理を作ったり、食べたり。おいしい料理とお酒があると、毎日が楽しくなるよ」

"In that case, cooking. You can make food and eat it. If you have delicious food and alcohol, every day is fun!"

「料理は、お腹がいっぱいになるだけで十分だ。
お酒も好きじゃない」

"As far as food goes, just getting full is enough. I don't like alcohol either."

いろいろな提案がありましたが、安田さんは、全部気に入りませんでした。

There were a lot of ideas, but Mr. Yasuda didn't like any of them.

そんな安田さんを見て、友達が言いました。

His friend looked at Mr. Yasuda and said,

「君の趣味がわかったよ」

"I know a good hobby for you."

「え？　それは何？」

"What? What's that?"

「君の趣味は、趣味を探すことだ」

"Your hobby is searching for a hobby."

The Long Staircase

長い階段

聡太の好きなものは、冷たいお茶と、友達の友美です。友美は、同じマンションの十五階に住んでいます。
嫌いなものは、牛乳と長い長い階段。

聡太は、友美に会いに、階段を上ります。聡太のうちは三階にありますから、毎日、たくさん汗をかきます。
「あら、聡太。今日もすごい汗ね」
「明日は、僕のうちに遊びに来てよ」
「嫌よ。聡太のうちは三階でしょう？　疲れるわ」
友美は、冷たいお茶をあげました。
「さあ、遊びましょう！　今日はトランプよ」
「う、うん！」

気がつくと夕方になっていました。うちに帰らなければならない時間です。
「じゃあね、また明日」
聡太はそう言って、近くのエレベーターに乗りました。階段は使いません。
「帰るときは、楽なんだけど」

聡太は、背伸びをして、エレベーターのボタンを押しました。

『8』階までのボタンは押すことができます。でも、『15』階のボタンは、届かないのです。

牛乳は嫌い。でも、早く大きくなりたい。

「嫌だけど、牛乳を飲まなければ」

聡太は、うちへ帰ると、鼻をつまんで牛乳を飲みました。

VOCABULARY LIST · 単語リスト

- マンション / *manshon* / apartment, apartment building

- 汗をかく / *aseokaku* / to sweat

- トランプ / *torampu* / card game with standard playing cards

- 気がつく / *kigatsuku* / to notice

- エレベーター / *erebētā* / elevator

- 楽 / *raku* / convenient, easy, comfortable

- 背伸びをする / *senobiosuru* / to stand on one's tip toes (lit. to stretch one's back)

- ボタン / *botan* / button

- 届く / *todoku* / to reach, to deliver

- 鼻をつまむ / *hanaotsumamu* / to plug one's nose

QUESTIONS・問題

次の問題から、正しい答えを一つ選んでください。

1. 聡太と友美は、どこで遊びましたか？[48]

   A. 聡太のうち

   B. 友美のうち

   C. 階段

2. 友美は、よく聡太のうちへ遊びに行きますか？[49]

   A. はい、行きます

   B. いいえ、行きません

---

[48] Q1. Where did Sota and Tomomi play?

[49] Q2. Does Tomomi often visit Sota's house to play?

3. どうして、聡太は、友美のうちへ行くとき、
階段を使いますか？[50]

   A.　汗をかくから

   B.　エレベーターがないから

   C.　エレベーターのボタンを押すことができないから

4. 聡太は、何が<u>できません</u>か？[51]

   A.　三階のボタンを押す

   B.　八階のボタンを押す

   C.　十五階のボタンを押す

5. どうして、聡太は、嫌いな牛乳を飲みましたか？
<u>合っていない</u>ものを選んでください。[52]

   A.　背が高くなりたいから

   B.　牛乳を好きになりたいから

   C.　友美のうちへ、楽に行きたいから

---

[50] Q3. Why does Sota use the stairs to get to Tomomi's house?

[51] Q4. What can Sota NOT do?

[52] Q5. Why did Sota drink milk, which he did not like? Please choose the option that does NOT match the details of the story.

ANSWERS・解答
かいとう

I. B.　友美のうち
ともみ

Tomomi's house.

2. B.　いいえ、行きません
い

No, she doesn't visit.

3. C.　エレベーターのボタンを押すことができないから
えれべーたー　　ぼたん　　お

Because he can't press the elevator button.

4. C.　十五階のボタンを押す
じゅうごかい　ぼたん　お

To press the button for the 15th floor.

5. B.　牛乳を好きになりたいから
ぎゅうにゅう　す

Because he wants to like milk.

THE LONG STAIRCASE WITH ENGLISH TRANSLATION

聡太の好きなものは、冷たいお茶と、友達の友美です。

Sota liked two things. Cold tea and his friend Tomomi.

友美は、同じマンションの十五階に住んでいます。

Tomomi lived in the same apartment as him on the fifteenth floor.

嫌いなものは、牛乳と長い長い階段。

He disliked two things. Milk and long, long stairs.

聡太は、友美に会いに、階段を上ります。

When he went to see Tomomi, he had to climb the stairs.

聡太のうちは三階にありますから、毎日、たくさん汗をかきます。

Sota lived on the third floor, so he sweated a lot everyday.

「あら、聡太。今日もすごい汗ね」

"Sota, you're all sweaty again!"

「明日は、僕のうちに遊びに来てよ」

"Tomorrow, come play at my house!"

「嫌よ。聡太のうちは三階でしょう？　疲れるわ」

"No way! You live on the third floor, right? I'd get tired."

友美は、冷たいお茶をあげました。

Tomomi gave him some cold tea.

「さあ、遊びましょう！　今日はトランプよ」

"Let's play something. How about card games, today?"

「う、うん！」

"Yes, yes!"

気がつくと夕方になっていました。うちに帰らなければ
ならない時間です。

Before he noticed, night had fallen. He had to go home.

「じゃあね、また明日」

"See you tomorrow!"

聡太はそう言って、近くのエレベーターに乗りました。

Sota said and got in the elevator.

階段は使いません。

He didn't use the stairs.

「帰るときは、楽なんだけど」

It's convenient for the way back.

聡太は、背伸びをして、エレベーターのボタンを押しました。

Sota stood on his tiptoes and pressed the button on the elevator.

『8』階までのボタンは押すことができます。

でも、『15』階のボタンは、届かないのです。

He could press the "8" button on the elevator, but he couldn't reach the "15."

牛乳は嫌い。でも、早く大きくなりたい。

He hated milk. But he wanted to grow bigger.

「嫌だけど、牛乳を飲まなければ」

"I hate it, but I gotta drink milk."

聡太は、うちへ帰ると、鼻をつまんで牛乳を飲みました。

Sota got back home, plugged his nose, and drank some milk.

落とし物

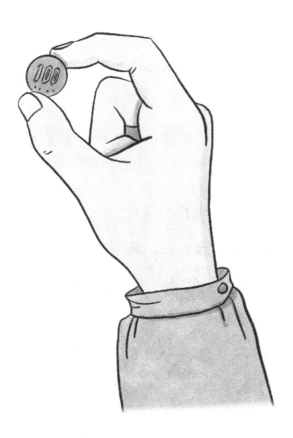

男の人は、毎日同じ時間に、同じ道で駅へ行きました。

その日の朝も、同じ時間、同じ道。

歩いていると、道に小さな光る物がありました。近くでよく見ると、それは一枚の百円玉でした。男の人は、その百円玉を拾って、ズボンのポケットに入れました。

近くに交番がありましたが、男の人は交番の方を全然見ないで歩きました。

次の日の朝、また同じ道に五百円玉が落ちていました。

男の人は五百円玉を拾うと、またズボンのポケットに入れました。

交番の前を通るとき、交番の方を少し見ました。

また次の日の朝、千円札が落ちていました。

男の人は、周りを見ました。誰もいません。

そして、すぐに千円札を拾って、ズボンのポケットに入れました。

交番の前を通るとき、今度は、下を見ながら、急いで歩いて行きました。

そして、また次の日。一万円札が落ちていました。

男の人は、一万円札を見ながら、しばらく立っていました。

「今、そこで拾いました」

男の人は、交番で若いお巡りさんに一万円札を渡しました。

「ありがとうございます。じゃあ、この紙に名前を書いてください」

お巡りさんは、紙とペンを渡しました。

男の人は、書き始めて、すぐに手が止まりました。

拾った金額……。

「どうしましたか?」

男の人は、ペンを置きました。そして、財布から千円札と五百円玉、そして百円玉を出しました。

「これも、そこの道で拾いました」と、男の人はお巡りさんを見て、言いました。

その目は、まっすぐできれいでした。

VOCABULARY LIST ・ 単語リスト

- 光る / *hikaru* / to be shiny, to shine
- 〜玉 / *dama* / 〜yen coin
- 拾う / *hirou* / to pick up
- ポケット / *poketto* / pocket
- 交番 / *kōban* / police box[53]
- 通る / *tōru* / to pass in front of
- 〜札 / *satsu* / 〜yen bill
- 周り / *mawari* / around
- しばらく / *shibaraku* / for a while
- お巡りさん / *omawarisan* / police officer
- 金額 / *kingaku* / amount (monetary)
- まっすぐ / *massugu* / honest, straight, straightforward, direct

---

[53] In Japan, there are little buildings that function as police stations scattered throughout the town. People often bring lost items there or report things to the police as necessary.

QUESTIONS・問題
<ruby>問題<rt>もんだい</rt></ruby>

<ruby>次<rt>つぎ</rt></ruby>の<ruby>問題<rt>もんだい</rt></ruby>から、<ruby>正<rt>ただ</rt></ruby>しい<ruby>答<rt>こた</rt></ruby>えを<ruby>一<rt>ひと</rt></ruby>つ<ruby>選<rt>えら</rt></ruby>んでください。

1. <ruby>男<rt>おとこ</rt></ruby>の<ruby>人<rt>ひと</rt></ruby>は、いつお<ruby>金<rt>かね</rt></ruby>を<ruby>拾<rt>ひろ</rt></ruby>いましたか？[54]

  A. <ruby>駅<rt>えき</rt></ruby>へ<ruby>行<rt>い</rt></ruby>くとき

  B. <ruby>駅<rt>えき</rt></ruby>へ<ruby>行<rt>い</rt></ruby>ったとき

2. どうして、<ruby>男<rt>おとこ</rt></ruby>の<ruby>人<rt>ひと</rt></ruby>は「<ruby>下<rt>した</rt></ruby>を<ruby>見<rt>み</rt></ruby>ながら、<ruby>急<rt>いそ</rt></ruby>いで<ruby>歩<rt>ある</rt></ruby>いて<ruby>行<rt>い</rt></ruby>きました」か？[55]

  A. <ruby>自分<rt>じぶん</rt></ruby>が<ruby>悪<rt>わる</rt></ruby>いことをしていると<ruby>思<rt>おも</rt></ruby>ったから

  B. もっとお<ruby>金<rt>かね</rt></ruby>が<ruby>落<rt>お</rt></ruby>ちていると<ruby>思<rt>おも</rt></ruby>ったから

  C. お<ruby>金<rt>かね</rt></ruby>を<ruby>拾<rt>ひろ</rt></ruby>って、うれしかったから

---

[54] Q1. When did the man pick up the money?

[55] Q2. Why did the man "下を見ながら、急いで歩いて行きました"?

3. どうして、お巡りさんは「どうしましたか？」と聞きましたか？[56]

    A. 拾った金額を忘れたから

    B. 男の人の手が止まったから

    C. 男の人にお金をあげたいと思ったから

4. 男の人は、「金額」のところに、いくら書きましたか？[57]

    A. 一万千六百円

    B. 一万円

    C. 千六百円

5. お話の内容と合っていないものは、どれですか？[58]

    A. 男の人は、小さな光る物を拾った

    B. 男の人は、本当のことを言った

    C. 男の人は、毎日交番へ行った

---

[56] Q3. Why did the officer ask "どうしましたか？"?

[57] Q4. How much did the man write in the "金額" section?

[58] Q5. Which one does NOT match the details of the story?

ANSWERS・解答
かいとう

---

1. A.　駅へ行くとき
えき　い

When going to the station.

2. A.　自分が悪いことをしていると思ったから
じぶん　わる　　　　　　　　　　　　おも

Because he thought he was doing something wrong.

3. B.　男の人の手が止まったから
おとこ ひと　て　と

Because the man's hand stopped.

4. A.　一万千六百円
いちまんせんろっぴゃくえん

Eleven thousand six hundred yen.

5. C.　男の人は、毎日交番へ行った
おとこ ひと　　　　まいにちこうばん　い

The man went to the police box every day.

THE LOST ITEM WITH ENGLISH TRANSLATION

男の人は、毎日同じ時間に、同じ道で駅へ行きました。

One man walked to the station at the same time along

the same road everyday.

その日の朝も、同じ時間、同じ道。

That morning too, it was the same time and the same

road.

歩いていると、道に小さな光る物がありました。

As he was walking, he saw a small shining object on the

road.

近くでよく見ると、それは一枚の百円玉でした。

When he looked at it closely, it was a 100-yen coin.

男の人は、その百円玉を拾って、ズボンの
ポケットに入れました。

The man picked up the 100-yen coin and put it in his

pocket.

近くに交番がありましたが、男の人は交番の方を
全然見ないで歩きました。

There was a police box nearby, but he didn't look in the direction of it at all and kept walking.

次の日の朝、また同じ道に五百円玉が落ちて[59]いました。

The next morning, there was a 500-yen coin on the same road.

男の人は五百円玉を拾うと、またズボンのポケットに入れました。

The man picked up the 500-yen coin and put it in his pocket.

交番の前を通るとき、交番の方を少し見ました。

He passed in front of the same police box and looked at it a little.

また次の日の朝、千円札が落ちていました。

The next morning, there was a 1,000 yen bill on the road.

男の人は、周りを見ました。誰もいません。

The man looked around. No one was there.

---

59 The word 落ちる literally means for drop something. In this case, the implication is the money was dropped on the ground and then forgotten.

そして、すぐに千円札を拾って、ズボンのポケットに入れました。

He picked up the 1,000-yen bill and put it in his pocket.

交番の前を通るとき、今度は、下を見ながら、急いで歩いて行きました。

He passed by the police box again. This time he looked down, hurriedly walking away.

そして、また次の日。一万円札が落ちていました。

And again, the next day. There was a 10,000-yen bill on the road.

男の人は、一万円札を見ながら、しばらく立っていました。

The man looked at the 10,000-yen bill and stood there for a while.

「今、そこで拾いました」

"I picked this up over there."

男の人は、交番で若いお巡りさんに一万円札を渡しました。

The man handed the 10,000-yen bill to the young police officer in the police box.

「ありがとうございます。じゃあ、この紙に名前を書いてください」

"Thank you very much. Please write your name on this paper."

お巡りさんは、紙とペンを渡しました。

The officer handed him a pen and paper.

男の人は、書き始めて、すぐに手が止まりました。

The man began to write but his hand stopped.

拾った金額……。

The amount of the money picked up.

「どうしましたか？」

"What's wrong?"

男の人は、ペンを置きました。

The man put his pen down.

そして、財布から千円札と五百円玉、そして
百円玉を出しました。

He took out the 1,000-yen bill, the 500-yen coin, and

the 100-yen coin from his wallet.

「これも、そこの道で拾いました」と、男の人はお巡り

さんを見て、言いました。

"I also picked this up on the road," he said as he looked

at the officer.

その目は、まっすぐできれいでした。

His eyes were honest and beautiful.

AFTERWORD

If you've made it this far, we sincerely hope that this book has helped you. Equally important is this: Did you enjoy reading it? Let us know which story you like the best by leaving a review. And hey, if you haven't yet, make sure you get your free gift! It's all part of your journey towards becoming a native Japanese speaker.

がんばれー！

REFERENCES

The Red Candle 赤い蝋燭

Original text: Nankichi Niimi

https://www.aozora.gr.jp/cards/000121/files/627_13466.html

The Mask マスク

Original text: Takoya Hayasaka

Dislikes 苦手なもの

Original text: Mitsuki Hachiga / Yumi Nishino

A Certain Medicine ある薬

Original text: Mitsuki Hachiga / Yumi Nishino

The Friendship Bracelet ミサンガ

Original text: Saya Onda

Japanese Cuisine 日本の料理

Original text: Takoya Hayasaka

Candy 飴だま

Original text: Nankichi Niimi

https://www.aozora.gr.jp/cards/000121/files/4723_13209.html

Hobby 趣味

Original text: Takoya Hayasaka

The Long Staircase 長い階段

Original text: Hagaki Fuyuno

The Lost Item 落とし物

Original text: Ayumu Sumio

ABOUT AUTHOR

<ruby>西野<rt>にしの</rt></ruby> <ruby>由美<rt>ゆみ</rt></ruby>

Yumi Nishino is Japanese, born and raised. Growing up, she has maintained an interest in studying English through reading English stories. A signature throughout her life has always been reading for enjoyment in both English and Japanese. Her favorite writers and inspirations include Shinichi Hoshi, Keigo Higashino, Kiyoshi Shigematsu, and Haruki Murakami.

It is also through stories that she shares her love for learners of Japanese. Asking questions such as "What kind of stories would readers find interesting?" and "How can we close the cultural distances between Japan and the rest of the world?" allows her to access the stories that are the perfect fit for potential readers, ensuring that there is enough content and context to make learning enjoyable. It is not only that, however, as she strives to locate the level differences of Japanese language learners and make the smaller bridges easier to cross, allowing them to reach for bigger and better things.

Mrs. Nishino herself continues to learn both English and Japanese, believing that language learning is a constant process. She thinks that learning new things can help her become better at creating the right stories and creating a better understanding for learners of Japanese. After graduating from Kyoto Sangyo University, she worked around the world before settling down in the United States. She currently lives in Texas with her husband and a small vegetable garden where squirrels often play.

Made in the USA
Monee, IL
14 November 2024

70130912R00085